Remember Jesus

52 Communion Thoughts and Meditations

By Don Lawrence

Most Christian Churches celebrate the Lord's Supper, or the Communion Service, on a regular basis. Some do so weekly, some monthly, others on a different schedule. The method of serving the Emblems varies from church to church. Some espouse Transubstantiation (the elements of the Lord's Supper are transformed into the actual flesh and blood of Christ, though not in appearance), others proclaim Consubstantiation (the elements of the Lord's Supper are spiritually the flesh and blood of Jesus, yet still the physical elements of the Lord's Supper), while others believe in a more figurative or symbolic approach of the celebration Emblems. Some churches invite congregants to come forward to be served. Others serve the congregants where they are seated. The methodologies of the Communion Service vary. But first and foremost, Communion is all about remembering Jesus. While instituting the Communion Service, Jesus said, "Do this in remembrance of me." (1 Corinthians 11:25). Of that, there is no debate.

This book contains fifty-two brief meditations or thoughts about the celebration of Communion, or the Lord's Supper. (Communion and Lord's Supper are used interchangeably throughout this book.) The meditations in this book are applicable for actual use during a church service, or may be used as a quick daily devotional. They are designed to enrich the time when we commune with God, individually or congregationally.

My prayer is that they will enrich you as you read them as much as they have enriched me during my writing of them.

Remembering Jesus,

Don Lawrence

Memories

Over the years I have presided over hundreds of funerals. At funerals and memorial services, we talk about the memories we have of our loved ones and how precious those memories are to us.

We share funny stories. We reflect upon special moments. We treasure the time together we had with our loved one.

Oftentimes, a video is made of the life of the one we are celebrating. The video, too, reminds us of our relationship, our time together, our cherished memories.

Special memories are one of the true blessings in life.

Let me ask you a question: At your funeral service, what do you want people to remember about you? What is something you hope they don't forget?

Here's another question: What do you think Jesus wants us to remember about Him?

The fact is, Jesus gave us the answer to that question. He had something that He wanted to be sure we would always remember. That is, the sacrifice he made on our behalf. After instituting the Lord's Supper, He said, "Do this in remembrance of me."

Luke 22:17 & 19
17   After taking the cup, Jesus gave thanks and said, "Take this and divide it among you.
19   And he took bread, gave thanks and broke it, and gave it to them, saying, "This is my body given for you; do this in remembrance of me."

There are many distractions in life. There are many concerns. There are many activities, responsibilities, tasks to do... Sometimes these things short-circuit our memories. They can draw our attention away from that which is most important.

Jesus didn't want that to happen. So he said, "Do this in remembrance of me."
The Lord's Supper provides us the opportunity to remember again what our Lord has done for us.

Before We Existed

In The Book of Revelation, chapter one verse four, and then repeated in verse eight, is the statement that Jesus, "Is and was and is to come." It also says that He is the, "Alpha and the Omega, the Beginning and the End."

In other words, Jesus has always existed. Before existence existed, He existed.

That is immensely important, especially when you look at what the Apostle Peter wrote:

1 Peter 1:18-20

18   For you know that it was not with perishable things such as silver or gold that you were redeemed from the empty way of life handed down to you from your forefathers,

19   but with the precious blood of Christ, a lamb without blemish or defect.

20   He was chosen before the creation of the world, but was revealed in these last times for your sake.

Before we were created, it was determined that Jesus Christ would die for us.

Our forgiveness was in place before we were even created. Our forgiveness was in place before our sins were ever committed.

Please think about this for a moment: Before we were created, God knew that we would sin. He knew that He would visit us in the person of Jesus Christ. He knew that He would give His life for our salvation. He knew all of the details about the horrific crucifixion: the scourging, the beatings, the crown of thorns, the nails in His wrists and ankles, the spear in His side... And yet, knowing all of this, He still created us. Isn't that incredible!

Ephesians 1:4, "For he chose us in him before the creation of the world to be holy and blameless in his sight..."

God knows things for eternity, but we forget things from last week!
God doesn't want us to forget the sacrifice Jesus made for us.
The emblems of the Communion Service are to remind us that God has always loved us.
The emblems are to remind us that God has always wanted us to be with Him in Heaven.
The emblems are to remind us that Jesus has made that possible.

Divine Fellowship

When we think of the concept of Christian fellowship, we tend to think of it in regards to our relationship with each other in the church. But let us not forget that there is another dimension of fellowship. That is, our fellowship with our Lord.

1 Corinthians 1:9, "God, who has called you into fellowship with his Son Jesus Christ our Lord, is faithful."

We are called to fellowship with Jesus. How cool is that! The root of the word communion is commune. We are to commune, or fellowship, with Jesus.

1 John 1:3, "We proclaim to you what we have seen and heard, so that you also may have fellowship with us. And our fellowship is with the Father and with his Son, Jesus Christ."

What a marvelous thing, to have such a relationship with the Creator of the universe.
We get to fellowship with the Lord, Himself!
The writer of the Book of Hebrews said, "Let us draw near to God with a sincere heart in full assurance of faith, having our hearts sprinkled to cleanse us from a guilty conscience and having our bodies washed with pure water." Hebrews 10:22

"Draw near to God." Divine fellowship!
But, how is that possible? We know that we all sin. We know that sin separates us from the Lord. So, how is such fellowship possible?

It's possible because of what Jesus did on the cross for us. And that's what communion is all about. His body was broken, His blood was shed, as a result of taking the punishment of our sins upon himself.

His body was broken - symbolized by the wafer we share. His blood was shed - symbolized by the juice we share.
Because of that which is represented by these emblems we share, we are also able to share fellowship with our Lord. Divine fellowship!

Life is in The Blood

We've seen it happen many times. A tragedy occurs and the Red Cross puts out a plea for blood donations.

It certainly was seen after the terrorist attacks on September 11, 2001.

Later that day and on into the next couple of days, the news reported about the long lines of people who were waiting to donate blood. Hundreds and hundreds and hundreds of people all across the country responded to the plea for blood donations.

In emergency situations, blood becomes critical. Obviously, blood is essential for life. The Bible itself teaches this elementary truth about life:

Leviticus 17:11, "For the life of a creature is in the blood..."

Blood is essential for life. Without blood you die. That's true physically. It's also true of your spiritual well-being.

Your sins are cleansed, your sins are washed away, by blood. Not your own blood. And not just anyone else's. But by the blood of Jesus Christ:

Ephesians 1:7, "In Christ we have redemption through his blood, the forgiveness of sins, in accordance with the riches of God's grace."

1 John 1:7, "But if we walk in the light, as he is in the light, we have fellowship with one another, and the blood of Jesus, his Son, purifies us from all sin."

Life is in the blood.

The Lord's Supper reminds that eternal life is also in the blood. The blood of Jesus.
The juice reminds us of Christ's blood, shed on the cross.
The bread reminds us that His body was broken, in sacrifice, for our salvation.

The Name of Jesus

In the Book of Acts, chapter 4, we read that the Apostles Peter and John healed a man. A critical part of this story is that this man was healed in the name of Jesus Christ. The name of Jesus was essential for his healing.

Acts 4:7 & 10
7 They had Peter and John brought before them and began to question them: "By what power or what name did you do this?"
10 ... "It is by the name of Jesus Christ of Nazareth...that this man stands before you healed."

He was healed by the name of Jesus Christ. But, he's not the only one. YOU also are healed in the name of Jesus Christ. The wounds of sin are healed by the blood of Jesus.

1 Peter 2:24, "He himself bore our sins in his body on the tree...by his wounds you have been healed."

The name of Jesus Christ is essential for your spiritual healing, for your spiritual well-being, for your eternal life.

Acts 10:43, "All the prophets testify about him that everyone who believes in him receives forgiveness of sins through his name."

It's not just the fact that someone died for you that you have eternal life, it's the fact that JESUS CHRIST died for you that you have eternal life. Jesus is the key.

1 John 2:12, "I write to you, dear children, because your sins have been forgiven on account of his name."

When you partake of the Lord's Supper, or the Communion Service, remember that it is not just anyone's body and blood that the emblems represent, it is specifically the body and blood of Jesus Christ.

It is the name of Jesus, it is the body and blood of Jesus that saves us!

Peace

It seems that the evening news regularly contains stories of bombings, shootings, and various forms of social unrest. Our hearts are certainly burdened as we watch the tragic events continue to happen around the world on a regular basis.

People around the world are crying out for peace, they are praying for peace, they are even having peace rallies. And yet, there continues to be a sad lack of peace in the world.

I am reminded of the words of the prophet Jeremiah:

"... 'Peace, peace,' they say, when there is no peace." Jeremiah 8:11

But then, the words of another prophet echo through the ages:

Isaiah 9:6, "For to us a child is born, to us a son is given, and the government will be on his shoulders. And he will be called Wonderful Counselor, Mighty God, Everlasting Father, Prince of Peace."

Among other things, this child is referred to as the "...Prince of Peace." Of course, the prophet speaks of Jesus. Years later, Jesus would state:

John 14:27, "Peace I leave with you; my peace I give you. I do not give to you as the world gives. Do not let your hearts be troubled and do not be afraid."

The ultimate peace is a peace that is eternal, a peace that is a Divine peace. That's exactly what Jesus offers. We read of this peace through Jesus in the Book of Colossians:

Colossians 1:19-20

19 For God was pleased to have all his fullness dwell in him,
20 and through him to reconcile to himself all things,
whether things on earth or things in heaven, by making peace
through his blood, shed on the cross.

The world will never know peace until it knows Jesus, the
Prince of Peace. It is man's sinfulness that has robbed us of
peace in the world. It is man's sinfulness that kills peace.

Colossians says that peace comes through the blood of
Jesus, shed on the cross. Because the blood of Jesus washes
away our sins, it cleanses us of our sinfulness. Only by the
blood of Jesus, is peace possible.

The emblems of the Lord's Supper remind us of the
sacrifice Jesus made in securing our eternal peace.

Those Guys

Over the years I have been asked a question many times. It goes something like this:

"If Jesus was God, if Jesus was all powerful, why did He allow those guys to kill Him?"

Why did He allow those guys to arrest Him?

Why did He allow those guys to beat Him up?

Why did He allow those guys to put a crown of thorns upon His head?

Why did He allow those guys to nail Him to a cross?

Why did He allow those guys to shove a spear into His side?

Why did He allow those guys to crucify Him?!

Please understand: Jesus did not die because of those guys. He died because of us guys! Those guys didn't take His life. He gave His life for us guys. Look at these words of Jesus:

John 10:17-18

17 "The reason my Father loves me is that I lay down my life-only to take it up again.

18 No one takes it from me, but I lay it down of my own accord..."

Why would He do so? He explained that, too.

John 15:13, "Greater love has no one than this, that he lay down his life for his friends."

One of the verses we often read when preparing for the Lords Supper is from the Gospel of Luke:

Luke 22:19, "And he took bread, gave thanks and broke it, and gave it to them, saying 'This is my body given for you; do this in remembrance of me.'"

We typically emphasize two things when looking at this verse. "This is my body..." The bread in the communion service represents the body of Jesus. "Do this in remembrance of me." We are to remember Jesus through these emblems.

But there is a third part of this verse, right between those two statements, which we often overlook. "Given for you..."

He said, "This is my body, given for you." Given for you guys. For us guys.

Let's remember that what He did on the cross He did because of love. That love specifically includes all of us guys!

Blood Disease

Why Jesus? Why does the Bible teach that Jesus Christ is the only way to heaven?

If you were diagnosed with a blood disease and the diagnosis is that you'd have to have a blood transfusion to live, and if the person sitting next to you has the same disease, a transfusion from him or her will do you no good. You must have a transfusion from someone who is disease free.

We've all been to the Great Physician for a checkup, and His diagnosis is that we all have the same blood disease. He calls it sin.

Romans 3:23, "For all have sinned and fall short of the glory of God."

Our only hope is someone who does not have this disease. Someone untainted by sin.
Someone sinless. Someone like Jesus. Concerning Jesus, the Apostle Paul wrote:

"God made Him who had no sin to be sin for us, so that in Him we might become the righteousness of God." 2 Corinthians 5:20

The Apostle Peter said, "He committed no sin, and no deceit was found in His mouth."
1 Peter 2:22

The Apostle John stated, "But you know that He appeared so that He might take away our sins. And in Him is no sin." 1 John 3:5.

In fact, He is our only hope, because Jesus Christ is the only one who never sinned.
His blood is the only blood untainted by sin.

Ephesians 1:7, "In Him we have redemption through His blood, the forgiveness of sins, in accordance with the riches of God's grace."

1 John 1:7, "But if we walk in the light, as He is in the light, we have fellowship with one another, and the blood of Jesus, His Son, purifies us from all sin."

When Jesus established the Lord's Supper, or the communion service, we read,
"Then He took the cup, gave thanks and offered it to them, saying, 'Drink from it, all of you. This is my blood of the covenant, which is poured out for many for the forgiveness of sins. I tell you, I will not drink of this fruit of the vine from now on until that day when I drink it anew with you in my Father's kingdom." Matthew 26:27-29

As you partake of the Lord's Supper, the juice you drink represents the pure, sinless, untainted, saving blood of Jesus.

Cleanse The Temple

In Matthew's gospel, shortly after Jesus entered Jerusalem, he went into the temple and cleansed the temple. Those who were cheating the people at the money tables he chased out. Those who were charging exorbitant prices for the sacrificial doves, he chased out.

He cleansed the temple. Jesus still wants to cleanse the temple. But now, YOU are that temple.

1 Corinthians 3:16, "Don't you know that you yourselves are God's temple and that God's Spirit lives in you?"

Jesus is still in the temple cleaning business. He wants to cleanse your temple. Will you allow Him access? What are some of the things He needs to chase out of your life? What are some of the sins He needs to sweep away? Paul repeats this thought three chapters later

1 Corinthians 6:19-20
19 Do you not know that your body is a temple of the Holy Spirit, who is in you, whom you have received from God? You are not your own;
20 you were bought at a price. Therefore, honor God with your body.

Cleansing the temple can be an expensive thing. There is a price to be paid. The Apostle Paul writes that you were bought with a price. The emblems of the Lord's Supper remind us of this. The bread and the juice remind us of the price paid. The bread symbolizes His body, broken on the cross. The juice symbolizes His blood, shed on the cross.

Why not allow the Lord full access as you commune with Him?

The Blood of the Lamb

One of the critical moments in the life of Moses, and also critical in the deliverance of Israel from slavery in Egypt, was the night of the Passover. Even to this day those of the Jewish faith celebrate the Passover.

On that evening, the angel of death went throughout Egypt and the firstborn male in every family died. However, for those Jewish families who had sacrificed an unblemished lamb, and then sprinkled the blood of that lamb on their doorposts, the angel of death passed over their home and they did not suffer the death that others suffered.

The blood was the sign; the blood was the key. That very same principle applies to all of us who have been covered by the blood of Jesus Christ.

Ephesians 1:7, "In him we have redemption through his blood, the forgiveness of sins, in accordance with the riches of God's grace."

That's why the Apostle Peter would write:

"For you know that it was not with perishable things such as silver or gold that you were redeemed from the empty way of life handed down to you from your forefathers, but with the precious blood of Christ, a lamb without blemish or defect." 1 Peter 1:18-19.

Saved by the blood of an unblemished lamb. Death passed over. Jesus is our lamb without blemish or defect.

The emblems of the Lord's Supper are to remind us of the blood and broken body of our Lord, Jesus Christ, the Lamb of God. The juice reminds us of his blood that was shed on the cross. The bread reminds us of his broken body.

Christ's Return

Discussions about Christ's return are always intriguing. Hundreds and hundreds of books have been written on the subject. Many movies have been made about it. The Bible teaches it in both the Old and New Testament. Jesus talked about it many times. Preachers preach about what we should do and what we shouldn't do until Christ returns.

The subject of Christ's return is even mentioned in Biblical teaching about communion. Do you know that? The Apostle Paul tied the celebration of the Lord's supper into the return of Christ.

1 Corinthians 11:26, "For whenever you eat this bread and drink this cup, you proclaim the Lord's death until he comes."

We are supposed to do this until Jesus returns. Christians have been doing this for about 2,000 years now! Every week when you do this, you continue on that great Christian legacy, that solemn tradition. Each week, millions and millions of Christians around the world faithfully remember the Lord Jesus through the emblems of the Lord's Supper.

We look back with heartfelt gratitude at what the Lord did for our salvation. The bread symbolizes the broken body of Jesus. The juice symbolizes the blood of Jesus. We look forward with great anticipation to his return.

Being faithful in the celebration of the Lord's Supper serves to remind us that we are to be faithful in all things as we wait for his return.

We say with the Apostle John, "Amen, Come Lord Jesus." Revelation 22:20.

Power Under Control

I don't know if you'll ever see a better control of anger than you see in Jesus. First of all, you need to understand His power:

John 18:3-6
3 So Judas came to the grove, guiding a detachment of soldiers and some officials from the chief priests and Pharisees. They were carrying torches, lanterns and weapons.
4 Jesus, knowing all that was going to happen to him, went out and asked them, "Who is it you want?"
5 "Jesus of Nazareth," they replied. "I am he," Jesus said. (And Judas the traitor was standing there with them.)
6 When Jesus said, "I am he," they drew back and fell to the ground.

Just His spoken word levels an entire detachment of soldiers, as well as the officials from the chief priests and Pharisees. Just the power of His word knocked them all flat.

During His arrest in the Garden of Gethsemane, Jesus told the Apostle Peter,

"Do you think I cannot call on my Father, and He will at once put at my disposal more that twelve legions of angels?" Matthew 26:53.

That's a formidable force!

In the next several hours, they would beat Jesus, flog Him, punch Him, kick Him, spit on Him, pluck out His beard, mock Him, call Him names, belittle Him, ridicule Him....and finally, crucify Him.

And Jesus never lost His temper. He put up with all of it, including death itself, for your salvation.

He didn't have to die. He willingly died. Because love is greater than anger. And God is love.

The emblems of the Lord's Supper are emblems of love.

That You May Know

Satan is the accuser; he attacks Christians through accusations.

Another way he does that is to tell you that you really aren't saved. He'll tell you that you really aren't forgiven. He'll tell you that you really aren't going to heaven.

He's wrong!

1 John 5:13, "I write these things to you who believe in the name of the Son of God so that you may know that you have eternal life."

Not that you hope - "that you may KNOW." Not just wishful thinking - "that you may KNOW." Not some pie-in-the-sky dream - "that you may KNOW."

How is it that you can KNOW? Because of His sacrifice on the cross.

Romans 8:1, "Therefore, there is now no condemnation for those who are in Christ Jesus."

Regardless of what satan whispers in your ear, you can know that there is no condemnation for those in Christ. You can know that you have eternal life.

It's not anything that you or I have done. It's everything that He has done. The emblems remind us of the atoning sacrifice of Jesus. The bread symbolizes His broken body. The juice symbolizes His spilled blood. Shed to wash away our sins.

God is Love

God is so multi-faceted, so complex, so vast, that it is impossible for our finite minds to come anywhere close to fully understanding his infinite existence.

However, if you knew absolutely nothing about God, but you learned about the death, burial, and resurrection of Jesus Christ, you would learn the most important thing about God.

You would learn of God's love. Specifically, you would learn of God's love for you.

Jesus said it this way:

John 15:13, "Greater love has no one than this, that he lay down his life for his friends."

In learning about God's love, you are learning about the essence of His being. The Apostle John explains the following:

"And so we know and rely on the love God has for us. God is love. Whoever lives in love lives in God, and God in him." 1 John 4:16.

"God is love." To learn of God's love is to learn of the core of who He is. Love doesn't merely describe God's existence; love IS God's existence! His love is pure. His love is unconditional. His love is beautiful. His love is perfect. And, fortunately for us, His love is not conditional upon anything we say or do.

Romans 5:8, "But God demonstrates his own love for us in this: While we were still sinners, Christ died for us."

"While we were still sinners." In spite of our sin. God is love. That love never wavers. It is most clearly seen on the cross. The bread of communion symbolizes His crucified body. The juice of communion symbolizes His shed blood. Together they remind us of His perfect love.

A Public Proclamation

There are many ways to speak out about Jesus, to bear testimony about your faith in Jesus Christ. Did you know that the Lord's Supper is a public confession of your faith in Jesus? It is a way to proclaim Jesus. When people see you observing the Lord's Supper, they are witnessing a proclamation of the sacrifice Jesus has made.

1 Corinthians 11:26, "For whenever you eat this bread and drink this cup, you proclaim the Lord's death until he comes."

The very act of taking communion is another form of witnessing about Jesus. If someone were to observe you taking communion, what would they see? Would they see someone connecting with Jesus? Would they see someone deep in prayer, in conversation with their Lord? Would they see someone with a grateful heart, a word of thanks upon your lips?

Or would they see someone distracted or hurried or bored? The writer of the Book of Hebrews stated:

"Therefore, since we are receiving a kingdom that cannot be shaken, let us be thankful, and so worship God acceptably with reverence and awe." Hebrews 12:28

As we partake of the emblems, let others see us taking it with reverence, with humility, with respect, with love and adoration of our Lord and Savior, Jesus.

Let others see us proclaim Jesus as we partake of the emblems.

Rich and Poor

The Apostle Paul makes a very interesting statement in his second letter to the church in the town of Corinth:

2 Corinthians 8:9, "For you know the grace of our Lord Jesus Christ, that though he was rich, yet for your sakes he became poor, so that you through his poverty might become rich."

Let's examine the second part of this verse:
"Though he was rich..." It doesn't get any better than Heaven. Jesus had the entire universe for his front yard! He had an incredible mansion in Heaven with hundreds of thousands of angels as his servants. The value of heaven is incalculable. We can't even begin to imagine how wonderful Jesus had it.

"...yet for your sakes he became poor..." Jesus left all of the riches and treasures of heaven. He was God, but became a man. Talk about a demotion! He gave all that up.

"...so that through his poverty..." Death on a cross is about as low as a man can get. Crucified like a common criminal. He not only gave up Heaven, He gave up life. He sacrificed everything for you. He became impoverished.

"... you might become rich..." He gives you true value. He gives you eternal worth. He gives you an inheritance that is beyond your wildest imagination. He is preparing a mansion in heaven for you like one you have never seen before.

Jesus cancels the debt of your sins and gives you the wealth of eternal life. That's what the cross is all about. Communion reminds us exactly what Jesus has done for us.

Perfect!

The Apostle Paul's goal was to help Christians become spiritually mature and Christlike; in fact, he says, "perfect" in Christ. Look at what he wrote,

Colossians 1:28, "We proclaim him, admonishing and teaching everyone with all wisdom, so that we may present everyone perfect in Christ."

That's the goal, to present everyone perfect in Christ. And yet, read this verse:

Hebrews 10:14, "By one sacrifice he has made perfect forever those who are being made holy."

So which is it? Are you already perfect, or are you being made perfect?

The answer is: Yes. You are perfect, while simultaneously being made perfect. How so?

Jesus is the atoning sacrifice for your sins. It's a done deal. You are forgiven. You have been given a status of perfection. But we don't always live up to what we have already been given. In fact, we rarely live up to that status.

Communion provides the opportunity to be reminded of what Jesus Christ has done for us.
By His sacrifice we have been made perfect.

It's also a time to be honest with ourselves and with the Lord and confess that we often fall short of that perfection. It's a chance to examine ourselves to see where we need to change some of our actions and attitudes so that they more accurately align with our status.

We don't have to create perfection within ourselves. It's already there! Christ has made us perfect. We just need to live up to that perfection.

The emblems of communion remind us of what the Lord has made of us. Perfection!

Unity

Unity is an essential ingredient in the life of the church family. Unity. Oneness. The key is the word "one." In Ephesians 4:4-6 we read of:
One Body.
One Spirit.
One Hope.
One Lord.
One Faith.
One Baptism.
One Lord and Father.

One. Our strength is when we view the body of Christ as one. While we are talking about unity and oneness, let's talk about THE ONE who makes unity possible.

2 Corinthians 5:14-15
14   For Christ's love compels us, because we are convinced that one died for all, and therefore all died.
15   And he died for all, that those who live should no longer live for themselves but for the one who died for them and was raised again.

The purpose of the Lord's supper is simply to remember the One who died for you.
You are one person. Although you are only one person, you are indeed a very important one to our Lord. So important, that he gave his life for you.
Through the emblems of the Lord's Supper, let us remember The One who died for you as one.

Grace and Justice

Isn't grace a great thing!? Someone once said, "God's grace is greater than man's disgrace."
God's grace and mercy are greater than our disgraceful sins. However, how does one reconcile grace and justice. Although God is merciful, He is also just.

2 Thessalonians 1:6, "God is just: He will pay back trouble to those who trouble you."

God is just. How is justice served if grace is extended? Is justice simply ignored? If God ignores justice can scripture truthfully say that God is just?
God's grace doesn't mean that God's justice is ignored. It means that God's justice was extended at the cross. Did you know that grace AND justice are brought together at the cross?

Romans 3:23-25
23   For all have sinned and fall short of the glory of God,
24   and are justified freely by his grace through the redemption that came by Christ Jesus.
25   God presented him as a sacrifice of atonement, through faith in his blood. He did this to demonstrate his justice...

We are saved by grace. But justice is still served in that Jesus took the punishment of our sins upon Himself. This happened at the cross.

The emblems of the Lord's Supper remind us of the harmony of grace and justice. The shed blood, the broken body…justice was served so that we can receive grace. Isn't grace a great thing!?

A Special Memory

Do you enjoy looking through old family photo albums? The birth of a child, family vacations, graduations, birthday parties, anniversaries, Christmas, Easter, school photos... Special memories are one of the true blessings in life.

Jesus knows that memories are indeed very special; He had something He wanted to be sure we would always remember. That is, the sacrifice he made on our behalf. After instituting the Lord's Supper, He said, "Do this in remembrance of me."

Luke 22:17 & 19
17   After taking the cup, he gave thanks and said, "Take this and divide it among you.
19   And he took bread, gave thanks and broke it, and gave it to them, saying, "This is my body given for you; do this in remembrance of me."

The Lord's Supper is kind of a "snapshot" of what Jesus did for us on the cross. It's a quick picture that reminds us of the sacrifice He made for us.
It's a picture of His love.
It's a picture of His death.
It's a picture of our salvation.
It's a picture of his body sacrificed.
It's a picture of his blood shed.

This "picture" is kept in a very unique photo album. The image is seen in the bread and juice of communion.

Through the emblems of communion, let's remember again what Jesus has done for us.

Redemption

There is a very interesting thing that happens at the end of the Book of Ruth. Widows in that society were very vulnerable. That is why Jewish law provided a way in which family members could care for them. Instead of the widow, and all she owned, falling into the hands of anybody who came along, a family member could purchase (or redeem) the property and thus assume responsibility for the widow. Basically, such a family member would become a "redeemer."

Ruth 4:6, "At this, the kinsman-redeemer said, 'Then I cannot redeem it because I might endanger my own estate. You redeem it yourself. I cannot do it.'"
Ruth 4:8-10
8 So the kinsman-redeemer said to Boaz, "Buy it yourself."...
9 Then Boaz announced to the elders and all the people, "Today you are witnesses that I have bought from Naomi all the property of Elimelech, Kilion and Mahlon.
10 I have also acquired Ruth the Moabitess, Mahlon's widow, as my wife, in order to maintain the name of the dead with his property, so that his name will not disappear from among his family or from the town records. Today you are witnesses!"

This is somewhat a foreshadowing of our situation. Ruth needed a redeemer. So do you! To keep you from falling into the hands of satan, you need a redeemer. Your redeemer is Jesus Christ.

Galatians 4:4-6
4   But when the time had fully come, God sent his Son, born of a woman, born under law,
5   to redeem those under law, that we might receive the full rights of sons.

Galatians 3:13, "Christ redeemed us from the curse of the law..."

In the time of Ruth, money was paid for redemption to take place. There was a redemption purchase price. There is also a purchase price for your redemption, but it isn't money. The Apostle Peter explains:

1 Peter 1:18-19
18   For you know that it was not with perishable things such as silver or gold that you were redeemed....
19   but with the precious blood of Christ, a lamb without blemish or defect.

The emblems of the Lord's Supper remind us of the purchase price paid for our redemption.

The Only Way

A relationship with God is only available through Jesus Christ. This is the clear teaching of scripture:

Acts 4:12, "Salvation is found in no one else, for there is no other name under heaven given to men by which we must be saved."

Jesus was not shy in stating this truth:

John 14:6, "Jesus answered, 'I am the way and the truth and the life. No one comes to the Father except through me.'"

But, WHY is that? Why IS Jesus the only way? Because Jesus is the only one would could die for your sins. Someone else might indeed die for you for any number of reasons, but their death could not take away your sins. Jesus is the only one who can do that. John the Baptist proclaimed this when he said:

John 1:29, "The next day John saw Jesus coming toward him and said, 'Look, the Lamb of God, who takes away the sin of the world!'"

The Apostle Paul wrote about this in his letter to Timothy:

1 Timothy 2:5-6
5   For there is one God and one mediator between God and men, the man Christ Jesus,
6   who gave himself as a ransom for all men-the testimony given in its proper time.

No religious leader, no religious system, no one else, nothing else can cleanse you of your sins. That's why Jesus is the only way of salvation. He is the sacrificial lamb who washes your sins away.

When you partake of the emblems of the Lord's Supper, remember again - The Way, The Truth and the Life: Jesus Christ.

Proof!

Three different times in the gospels Jesus brought a person back to life. Think about that for a minute. They were dead! He didn't use the electric paddles or CPR or any medication. He simply spoke a word, and though they were dead, they came back to life.

It's all proof that Jesus is who He claimed to be! He is our Lord and Savior!! Think about it: you are placing your eternal destination on a belief in a guy named Jesus. There's a lot at stake. Jesus understood that. And he was willing to offer proof.

John 2:18-22
18 Then the Jews demanded of him, "What miraculous sign can you show us to prove your authority to do all this?"
19 Jesus answered them, "Destroy this temple, and I will raise it again in three days."
20 The Jews replied, "It has taken forty-six years to build this temple, and you are going to raise it in three days?"
21 But the temple he had spoken of was his body.
22 After he was raised from the dead, his disciples recalled what he had said. Then they believed the Scripture and the words that Jesus had spoken.

Jesus said, "You want proof? Kill my body. I'll bring it back to life in three days!"

Jesus offered his own life as proof that He had power over death. He was killed, He was buried, and three days later He was resurrected. And there were hundreds of witnesses to this fact!

The emblems of the Lord's Supper remind us of His death, and thus, remind us of the proof he offered.

Reflect again on your eternal destiny and the One who makes it all possible the next time you partake of the emblems.

Darkness and Light

I find it interesting, that as Jesus Christ was hanging on the cross, at the moment of his death, darkness covered the entire world.

Luke 23:44-46
44 It was now about the sixth hour, and darkness came over the whole land until the ninth hour,
45   for the sun stopped shining. And the curtain of the temple was torn in two.
46 Jesus called out with a loud voice, "Father, into your hands I commit my spirit." When he had said this, he breathed his last.

Among other things: Death is darkness. Jesus came to destroy death. He came to destroy darkness. In fact, Jesus referred to himself as the, "Light of the world."

John 8:12, "When Jesus spoke again to the people, he said, 'I am the light of the world. Whoever follows me will never walk in darkness, but will have the light of life.'"

Isn't it interesting that Christ's resurrection coincided with sunrise.

Luke 24:1-3, "On the first day of the week, very early in the morning, the women took the spices they had prepared and went to the tomb. They found the stone rolled away from the tomb, but when they entered, the did not find the body of the Lord Jesus."

It was at sunrise that his followers were told that Jesus had been resurrected.
Darkness at His death. Light at His resurrection.

As you contemplate the darkness of death, remember that Jesus conquered death, and thus ultimately also conquered darkness. In Jesus there is eternal light and eternal life!

Slavery to Freedom

The Passover was a key part of Israel's deliverance out of slavery in Egypt and into freedom.

God created the Jewish Passover Celebration because he wanted the nation of Israel to never, ever forget how he delivered them from slavery.

Slavery. Freedom. The whole purpose of Jesus' death on the cross was to deliver us from slavery. The Bible teaches that apart from Christ, we are slaves to sin.

Romans 6:6, "For we know that our old self was crucified with him so that the body of sin might be done away with, that we should no longer be slaves to sin."

Although we were slaves to sin, we have been set free from that slavery to sin. We don't have to sin. We can resist it!

Nor do we have to suffer the consequences of our sin: death. Jesus has freed us from sin and its eternal consequences.

Romans 6:22, "But now that you have been set free from sin ..."

That freedom was accomplished through Jesus' death on the cross. He was the sacrifice for our sins.

Just as God did not want the nation of Israel to ever forget what He did for them in Egypt,
the Lord doesn't want us to ever forget what He did for us on the cross.

He said, "...do this in remembrance of me." Luke 22:19.

Let us always remember our deliverance from slavery to sin into freedom from sin, through the sacrifice of Jesus Christ.

The Ultimate Peacemaker

Sometimes a peacemaker is needed. A couple may go to a counselor if they are at an impasse in their relationship. A parent may need to intercede to settle an argument between siblings. Some companies may have to go to court or arbitration to reach a settlement in a dispute. Police officers may be called to a situation to maintain the peace.

Matthew 5:9, "Blessed are the Peacemakers, for they will be called sons of God."

These words in Matthew's Gospel were spoken by the ultimate Peacemaker: Jesus Christ. Years later, the Apostle Paul would write:

Colossians 1:21, "Once you were alienated from God and were enemies in your minds because of your evil behavior."

We were alienated from God. We were not at peace with God. However, the previous two verses say:

Colossians 1:19-20 "For God was pleased to have all his fullness dwell in him, and through him to reconcile to himself all things, whether things on earth or things in heaven, by making peace through his blood, shed on the cross."

"Making peace." The Peacemaker. How? The verse concludes by saying, "Through His blood, shed on the cross."

The emblems of the Lord's Supper serve to remind us that Jesus' blood was shed and that his body was broken for us, so that we can be at peace with God.

Let us never forget Christ's sacrifice. And let us remember that precious relationship we have with our Heavenly Father because of what Jesus has done for us.

Thank You

In the Gospel of Luke, chapter seventeen, we read of the time Jesus healed ten lepers. After being healed, only one of the ten came back to say "thank you" to Jesus. Jesus then asked, "Where are the other nine?"

Do you sometimes get so busy with life that you forget to simply thank the Lord for the daily blessings he bestows upon you?

The celebration of the Lord's Supper is an opportunity for each of us to take a moment to say "thank you" to the Lord, not only for our daily blessings, but for our ultimate blessing.

In fact, consider these words of the Apostle Paul:

1 Corinthians 10:16, "Is not the cup of thanksgiving for which we give thanks a participation in the blood of Christ? And is not the bread that we break a participation in the body of Christ?"

The Apostle uses the expression, "…the cup of thanksgiving for which we give thanks…" And look at what Jesus Himself said while instituting the Lord's Supper:

Matthew 26:26-28
26   While they were eating, Jesus took bread, gave thanks and broke it, and gave it to his disciples, saying, "Take and eat; this is my body."
27   Then he took the cup, gave thanks and offered it to them, saying, "Drink from it, all of you.
28   This is my blood of the covenant, which is poured out for many for the forgiveness of sins.

The Apostle Paul said that it is an expression of Thanksgiving. Jesus gave thanks while establishing it. The Lord's Supper is a celebration of thanks.

Is there anything for which we should be more thankful than our salvation?
Is there anyone to whom we owe a greater debt of thanks than our Lord and Savior Jesus Christ?

Healed

In the Gospels we read of many different miracles of Jesus. We read of many people who were healed by Jesus. Jesus did lots of miracles. He did lots of healings.

By far, the most important healing is what He did on the cross. Jesus' sacrifice on the cross was all about healing. Only this time, WE are the ones who receive that miracle!

This healing was prophesied in the Old Testament:

Isaiah 53:5, "But he was pierced for our transgressions, he was crushed for our iniquities; the punishment that brought us peace was upon him, and by his wounds we are healed."

The prophet stated that we are healed by Christ's wounds from his crucifixion. The Apostle Peter also spoke of it:

1 Peter 2:24, "He himself bore our sins in his body on the tree, so that we might die to sins and live for righteousness; by his wounds you have been healed."

The Apostle Peter, too, states that we are healed by the wounds of Christ. How so? You have a spiritual disease called sin. We all do. Jesus took the punishment for our sins upon Himself. It was at the cross that Jesus healed that sin disease.

The emblems of the Lord's Supper remind us of the personal sacrifice Jesus made to bring about our healing.

Does God love you?

Do you ever wonder if God loves you?
When you think about the sins you have committed?
When you think about the way you have treated some people?
When you think about some of the language you have used?
When you think about some of the lustful thoughts you have harbored?
When you think about the forgiveness you have withheld from others?
When you think of your lack of compassion and caring for others?
When you think about...?

If you ever wonder how much God loves you, remember the cross. If you ever wonder how valuable you are to God, remember the cross. If you ever wonder how far God is willing to go to have a relationship with you, remember the cross.

Your salvation wasn't free! You came with a price tag.

1 Corinthians 6:20, "You were bought at a price. Therefore, honor God with your body."

The cost of your salvation was the life of Jesus Christ.

1 Peter 1:18-19
18   For you know that it was not with perishable things such as silver or gold that you were redeemed from the empty way of life handed down to you from your forefathers,
19   but with the precious blood of Christ, a lamb without blemish or defect.

In God's eyes, you are worth dying for. We are reminded of this each time we participate in the Lord's Supper.

Let us commune with the Lord in a manner that is reflective of our deepest appreciation of what He did for each of us on the cross.

Blood Poured Out

If one is traveling across the desert, water is essential. Those who live in the dessert do their best to conserve water. Water is not to be wasted.

Others have water in abundance and so they tend to take it for granted. But where water is scarce, it is protected, it is shielded, it is taken care of. In fact, it is cherished. You wouldn't want to accidently pour it out. The last thing you want to do is spill your water.

Water isn't the only thing that can be spilled. Sometimes blood is spilled. Sometimes, intentionally. Sometimes, accidently. Blood, too, can be poured out.

Jesus used the expression "poured out" when discussing what happened to his blood during the crucifixion.

Matthew 26:28, Jesus said, "This is my blood of the covenant, which is poured out for many for the forgiveness of sins."

Jesus' blood was shed on the cross so that our sins could be forgiven. There was no accident involved. It was intentional. By those who murdered him, but also, by Jesus Himself. He willingly allowed his blood to be spilled, to be poured out for our salvation. Let us not take this for granted. Let this act not be wasted. Let us cherish what he has done.

In the communion service, the juice reminds us of his blood being shed, the bread reminds us that his body was broken.

Let us cherish what Jesus has done for us on the cross.

An Examined Life

Plato once wrote, "An unexamined life is not worth living." We go to our physician for a physical exam. But who do you go to for a spiritual checkup?

When was the last time you examined your attitudes?

When was the last time you examined your spiritual disciplines, such as Bible reading, worship attendance, Christian service?

When was the last time you examined your prayer life?

When was the last time you examined the way that you treat others?

When was the last time you examined your motives?

When was the last time you examined your integrity?

When was the last time you examined your morality?

When was the last time you examined your priorities in life?

When was the last time you did an honest examination of your life?

Partaking in The Lord's Communion provides the opportunity for each of us to examine our own life. In fact, it's not just an opportunity, we are instructed to do so.

While discussing the Lord's Supper, the Apostle Paul wrote:

1 Corinthians 11:28, "A man ought to examine himself before he eats of the bread and drinks of the cup."

The Biblical instruction is that we should examine ourselves during this special time of communing with the Lord.

As we remember Jesus' life and death, let us use that as the background from which we examine our own lives.

Reverence

Reverence. What exactly does that word mean? It certainly would include the aspect of respect. A sense of awe is a key ingredient of reverence. So are such things as humility, honor, adoration and esteem. Reverence is seen in more than our attitude. It is also seen in our actions and conduct when in the presence of the one to whom reverence is shown.

If ever there was an appropriate time to be reverent, it is during the serving of the Lord's Supper.

The Apostle Paul addressed this issue when he wrote:

1 Corinthians 11:27, "Therefore, whoever eats the bread or drinks the cup of the Lord in an unworthy manner will be guilty of sinning against the body and blood of the Lord."

The writer of the Book of Hebrews said:

Hebrews 12:28, "Therefore, since we are receiving a kingdom that cannot be shaken, let us be thankful, and so worship God acceptably with reverence and awe, for our 'God is a consuming fire.'"

With reverence and awe. Communion provides the opportunity for both. A time to pray. A time to be still. It's not a time to whisper to your neighbor. It's a time to whisper a prayer to God.

Let us with reverence and awe remember the sacrifice Jesus has made for us as we worship him by participating in the Holy Communion.

Perfect Friendship

Do you have any friends who would literally lay down their life for you? That's something that is easy to say, but when push comes to shove, would they really be willing to die for you?

Let's turn it around. Do you have any friends for whom you would be willing to die? Honestly? Literally? Really?

Jesus is that kind of friend. Jesus gave His life for you. Jesus gives you the gift of friendship.

John 15:13, "Greater love has no one than this, that he lay down his life for his friends."

Love is easy to talk about. Perhaps, too easy. But as the saying goes, actions speak louder than words.

Romans 5:8, "But God demonstrates his own love for us in this: While we were still sinners, Christ died for us."

God didn't just say he loves you. He proved it on the cross. His love is perfect. His friendship is perfect.

The emblems of the Lord's Supper remind us of the kind of friend Jesus is. He died for us. He offers you the gift of his friendship.

The depth of that friendship is reflected in the emblems of the Lord's Supper. The bread reminds us that His body was broken for us. The juice reminds us that His blood was shed for the forgiveness of our sins.

Purple Heart

It is always an honor to sit and talk with veterans. They have some fascinating stories to share. They have some heartbreaking stories to share. They have some heroic stories to share.

Many veterans have various medals and pins they have been awarded for different reasons. One of the most respected and most recognizable is the Purple Heart.

The Purple Heart is given to those who have been injured or killed in the line of duty. To those who have been wounded or have died.

The Purple Heart medal is an emblem to remind us of the sacrifice a Veteran has made on our behalf.

In a way, the emblems of the Communion Service are like a Purple Heart. They remind us of the sacrifice our Lord made on our behalf. They remind us that He was injured, that He was wounded, in fact, that He gave His life. The bread of communion is like a medal, reminding us that Christ's body was broken for us. The juice of communion is like a medal, reminding us that Christ's blood was shed for us.

Matthew 26:26-28
26   While they were eating, Jesus took bread, gave thanks and broke it, and gave it to his disciples, saying, "Take and eat; this is my body."
27   Then he took the cup, gave thanks and offered it to them, saying, "Drink from it, all of you. 28   This is my blood of the covenant, which is poured out for many for the forgiveness of sins.

Let us not forget the sacrifice of our Lord and Savior, Jesus Christ.

The Lamb of God

As you know, Jesus is referred to as the lamb of God in scripture. In fact, in the book of Revelation, more than 30 times Jesus is referred to as the lamb. In the Gospel of John, we read:

John 1:29, "The next day John (The Baptist) saw Jesus coming toward him and said, 'Look, the Lamb of God, who takes away the sin of the world!'"

Why the lamb symbolism? It was one of the animals used in the Old Testament as a sin offering. When they sinned, they could have their sins forgiven by bringing a sin offering to the temple.

The problem with that is that they were guilty of their sin until they made the sin offering.

And after making the sin offering, as soon as they sinned again, they were guilty again. They remained in their sin until they were able to make another sin offering. And so on and on the cycle continued.

Jesus changed all that.

Hebrews 10:10, "...We have been made holy through the sacrifice of the body of Jesus Christ once for all."

"Once for all." Jesus' sacrifice for your sins never has to be repeated. His sacrifice is permanent. The sins of your past, the sins of your future, forgiven, once for all.

Romans 8:1, "Therefore, there is now no condemnation for those who are in Christ Jesus."

As you partake of the emblems, remember the lamb of God, who takes away the sins of the world.

Just One

Someone once said that even if you were the only person on the planet, Jesus would have given his life to save you. He still would have endured the cross. He still would have suffered.
He still would have bled. He still would have died. Even for one, just one, he would have left heaven to find you.

Jesus explains this truth when he stated the following:

Luke 15:4-6
4 "Suppose one of you has a hundred sheep and loses one of them. Does he not leave the ninety-nine in the open country and go after the lost sheep until he finds it?
5 And when he finds it, he joyfully puts it on his shoulders
6 and goes home. Then he calls his friends and neighbors together and says, 'Rejoice with me; I have found my lost sheep.'"

Jesus is the great shepherd. He left heaven and came to earth to save those he loves so much. Even if you were the only one on the planet, he would still have done it. And, he rejoices with the angels in heaven as each individual turns to him.

In verse 10 of Luke 15, Jesus goes on to say:

Luke 15:10, "In the same way, I tell you, there is rejoicing in the presence of the angels of God over one sinner who repents."

God loves you as an individual. He loves you personally. He knows everything there is to know about you. Jesus died on the cross so that you could have a personal relationship with Him.

The emblems of the Lord's Supper remind us just how much God desires for you to know him the way he knows you.

Be Still

I like what Mother Teresa said, "God rarely is found in the midst of noise and restlessness; instead, He is the friend of silence."

Does noise describe your existence? The television, the radio, the kids, the traffic, the phone, the crowds, the office...

Is silence a rare reality in your life? Consider the words of the psalmist:

Psalm 37:7, "Be still before the LORD and wait patiently for him..."

Psalm 46:10, "Be still, and know that I am God..."

Be still!? How? Where? When?

There's so much to do. Deadlines, appointments, meetings, shopping, yard work, laundry, house work, projects, kids' activities, church activities...

Who has time to be still? Where can silence be found?

How often do you have a moment of peace? A moment of silence? A moment to tune out the world and all of its concerns? A moment to focus wholeheartedly and completely upon God?

The Lord's Supper provides us the opportunity to be still, to be silent, to commune with the Lord. Don't rush through it! Bask in it. Relax in it. Engage the Lord through it.

Let us appreciate the moment when we come before our Lord, remembering through the emblems of the Lord's Supper what He has done for us.

Born Again

Jesus calls us to be born again.

John 3:3, "In reply Jesus declared, 'I tell you the truth, no one can see the kingdom of God unless he is born again.'"

This new birth is reflected in the words of the Apostle Paul:

2 Corinthians 5:17, "Therefore, if anyone is in Christ, he is a new creation; the old has gone, the new has come!"

Once you have been born again, once you have experienced a spiritual birth, once you are a new creation, you will live in conflict. The conflict is between the old you and the new you. The conflict is between the physical you and the spiritual you. The conflict is between the worldly you and the heavenly you.

It eventually gets down to which will have the priority in your life: physical or spiritual?

Hebrews 9:14, "How much more, then, will the blood of Christ, who through the eternal Spirit offered himself unblemished to God, cleanse our consciences from acts that lead to death, so that we may serve the living God!"

The Lord's Supper reminds us that, through the Holy Spirit, the blood of Christ cleanses us and makes it possible for this spiritual birth. We can only be born again because of what Jesus did on the cross. We can only go to Heaven, we can only have eternal life because of Jesus' sacrifice.

It all starts at the cross. The emblems of the Lord's Supper remind us not only of Jesus' death, but of our spiritual lives.

Justice, Mercy, Grace

Justice means you get what you deserve.
Grace means you get what you don't deserve.
Mercy means you don't get what you do deserve.

God gives us mercy. But that doesn't mean that justice isn't served. You see, justice must be served because the scripture says God is a just God.

Justice means you get what you deserve. So God took care of justice, in that, He gave to Jesus what we deserve.

Romans 3:25-26
25   God presented him as a sacrifice of atonement, through faith in his blood. He did this to demonstrate his justice...
26   he did it to demonstrate his justice at the present time, so as to be just and the one who justifies those who have faith in Jesus.

Justice was served at the cross. Mercy means we don't get the punishment we deserve.
Instead of punishment, we get eternal life.

1 Peter 1:3, "Praise be to the God and Father of our Lord Jesus Christ! In his great mercy he has given us new birth into a living hope through the resurrection of Jesus Christ from the dead."

Before mercy could be extended, justice had to be served. The next time you partake of the emblems, praise God for His mercy, but also remember the price that was paid so that justice could be served.

Faithful

God is faithful to keeping his covenant.

Deuteronomy 7:9, "Know therefore that the Lord your God is the faithful God, keeping his covenant of love to a thousand generations...."

A covenant is a promise. In other words, God keeps His promises. He does not break his covenant. Jesus made a promise to all of his followers:

John 14:2-3
2   In my Father's house are many rooms; if it were not so, I would have told you. I am going there to prepare a place for you.
3   And if I go and prepare a place for you, I will come back and take you to be with me that you also may be where I am.

Jesus has promised to come back. His return will be a testimony to his faithfulness.
In fact, this is such a sure thing, that one of His names is Faithful.

Revelation 19:11, "I saw heaven standing open and there before me was a white horse, whose rider is called Faithful and True..."

Hebrews 10:23, "Let us hold unswervingly to the hope we profess, for he who promised is faithful."

Jesus keeps his promises. He promised to come back. He will be faithful to that promise.
You are to be faithful until He returns.

Jesus said, "...Be faithful, even to the point of death, and I will give you the crown of life." Revelation 2:10.

One of the demonstrations of your faithfulness is your participation in the Lord's Supper.

1 Corinthians 11:26, "For whenever you eat this bread and drink this cup, you proclaim the Lord's death until he comes."

How long should the church continue to share the Lord's Supper? We will do so faithfully until He returns.

Remember

It is said that more long distance phone calls are made on Mother's Day than any other day of the year. It also said that more COLLECT calls are placed on Father's Day than any other day of the year! And every Father I know would say, "That's okay. It's just nice to be remembered."

Do you have fond memories of your father and/or mother? How about your grandparents?
Perhaps you have special memories about someone else who was a vital part of your upbringing. It's nice to be remembered.

Jesus made a comment about being remembered. Jesus said, "Do this in remembrance of me." He was talking about the Lord's Supper. We do it to remember Jesus.

Luke 22:17-19
17   After taking the cup, he gave thanks and said, "Take this and divide it among you.
18   For I tell you I will not drink again of the fruit of the vine until the kingdom of God comes."
19   And he took bread, gave thanks and broke it, and gave it to them, saying, "This is my body given for you; do this in remembrance of me."

Partaking of the Lord's Supper is kind of like your phone call home. And don't worry about calling collect, He's already paid the bill!
"Lord, just calling to say I remember. I haven't forgotten. I love you. Thanks."

The Blood of Jesus

There is only one reason our prayers work. That reason is Jesus. Specifically, it is what Jesus did on the cross. If not for what Jesus did on the cross our prayers would not be answered. They wouldn't even be heard by God.

But Jesus has made it possible for us to enter into God's presence and commune with Him.
Jesus has made it possible for us to enter into God's presence and converse with Him.

Hebrews 10:19, "Therefore, brothers, since we have confidence to enter the Most Holy Place by the blood of Jesus..."

The blood of Jesus. It washes away our sins. It washes us clean. Without Christ's sacrifice on the cross, our sins separate us from God. A relationship with God is impossible without Jesus.
It is Christ's shed blood on the cross that makes the relationship possible, that makes God accessible to us, and that makes prayer work.

The blood of Jesus. It is what we remember when we partake of the Lord's Supper. The bread reminds us of his broken body. The juice reminds us that his blood was shed.
It is that very sacrifice which makes it possible for us to enter into a relationship with God.
It is through that sacrifice that our prayers are heard.

A Free Gift

Our salvation is a free gift. That is, free to us. The reason it is free to us is because Jesus already paid the price for our salvation. That's why our salvation is referred to as a gift.

Ephesians 2:8, "For it is by grace you have been saved, through faith-and this not from yourselves, it is the gift of God."

If you go to the store and buy a gift for someone, you will be given a receipt. When you give that gift to someone, it cost them nothing. It's a free gift. But you paid for the gift. The receipt will tell you the price of the gift.

Your salvation is a free gift to you. But Jesus paid for it. The emblems of the Lord's Supper are the receipt of God's gift to us, our salvation. You can look at the receipt and see the cost.
The bread represents the body of Christ.
The juice represents the blood of Christ.
The body and the blood of Jesus. The price of your salvation.

Romans 6:23, "For the wages of sin is death, but the gift of God is eternal life in Christ Jesus our Lord."

Realizing the cost of the gift only deepens our appreciation of it.

Love is the Key

One of the key components of a good marriage is self-denial. Putting your spouse before yourself. This is not always an easy thing to do. It goes against our self-centered human nature.

But it is somewhat an indicator of the depth of the love a person has. Love will empower you to do what self-centeredness would keep you from doing. Love is the key.

This self-denial, putting your spouse first attitude, was of course indicative of Christ's love for you. In fact, His love for us is to be an example of how we should love our spouse.

Look at Ephesians 5:25, "Husbands, love your wives, just as Christ loved the church and gave himself up for her."

Jesus gave himself up, on the cross, for us because of his tremendous love for us. He gave himself up by dying for us, because of his love for us.

Romans 5:8, "But God demonstrates his own love for us in this: While we were still sinners, Christ died for us."

Love is the key.

1 John 4:10, "This is love: not that we loved God, but that he loved us and sent his Son as an atoning sacrifice for our sins."

The emblems of the Lord's Supper remind us of that perfect love.

Christmas and Easter

He was just a baby. A baby laid in a manger at his birth. A baby they would not make room for in the inn. A baby who was vulnerable. A baby who needed to be cared for: to be fed and changed and held and clothed.

He was just a baby.

But He wasn't really JUST a baby. He was God incarnate. God in human form.

Colossians 2:9, "For in Christ all the fullness of the Deity lives in bodily form"

All the fullness of the Deity. All of God. God incarnate. He wasn't just a baby. He was the Messiah, the Savior, the deliverer, the conqueror... he was God.

You see, the problem is that it is easy to forget that, in fact, He wasn't JUST a baby.

It's so easy to get caught up in all the pageantry, in the nativity, in the celebration, in the many Christmas activities... that one forgets.

We get so caught up in Christmas that we forget about Easter. We get so focused on His cradle that sometimes we forget about the cross.

And He didn't come here for the cradle, He came here for the cross. Easter reminds us of this truth. Jesus, referring to himself as the Son of Man, said:

Matthew 20:28, "Just as the Son of Man did not come to be served but to serve, and to give his life as a ransom for many."

It is Easter that helps us keep Christmas in perspective. Likewise, the celebration of the Communion service helps us to keep Christmas in perspective. It helps us to remember the cross. It helps us to remember the death of Jesus, as well as His glorious resurrection!

An Unworthy Manner

Communion, the Lord's Supper, should be a time of silent introspection and silent reflection and silent self-examination.

1 Corinthians 11:27-28
27   Therefore, whoever eats the bread or drinks the cup of the Lord in an unworthy manner will be guilty of sinning against the body and blood of the Lord.
28   A man ought to examine himself before he eats of the bread and drinks of the cup.

The Apostle Paul chastises Christians who partake of the communion service in an unworthy manner. We don't want to be guilty of doing that. But, what is an unworthy manner?

It all gets back to the basic reason Jesus established the communion service. He said, "This is my body...this is my blood."

That's why Paul said if you partake in an unworthy manner, you sin against the "body" and "blood" of the Lord. Anything that diverts your attention from the body and blood of the Lord is unworthy.

You can't whisper to someone sitting next to you, and still focus on the body and blood of the Lord. You can't work on your grocery shopping list, and still focus on the body and blood of the Lord. You can't think about this afternoon's ball game and sill focus on the body and blood of the Lord.

Paul also said a man should examine himself.

For example: Determine what sins in your life need to be confessed before the Lord. Determine what sins in your life you need to confess to whomever you may have sinned against. And then remember that your sins are what the broken body and shed blood of the Lord are all about.

Let us silently, introspectively, humbly remember our Lord's sacrifice when we partake of the emblems of the Lord's Supper.

Sacred

The concept of being a part of God's Holy temple is really very profound. It should not be taken lightly. It's a sacred thing:

1 Corinthians 3:17, "If anyone destroys God's temple, God will destroy him; for God's temple is sacred, and you are that temple."

Once you have received Jesus Christ as your Lord and Savior, the Holy Spirit takes up residence within you. The Bible says that makes your body sacred to God.

You are supposed to be sacred. You are supposed to be holy. Obviously, that's got to have an impact upon your lifestyle:

2 Corinthians 7:1, "Since we have these promises, dear friends, let us purify ourselves from everything that contaminates body and spirit, perfecting holiness out of reverence for God."

Now, some think, "I don't feel exactly sacred. Sometimes I think bad things, sometimes I say bad things, I have certainly done some bad things...sacred? Me?"

And yet, in God's eyes, you are sacred. You have been made holy.

The emblems of the Lord's Supper remind us of what it took to purify us, to perfect us, to make us Holy, to make us sacred. It took the blood of Jesus to clean us up.

1 John 1:7, "But if we walk in the light, as he is in the light, we have fellowship with one another, and the blood of Jesus, his Son, purifies us from all sin."

The juice of communion reminds us of Jesus' blood. The bread of communion reminds us of Jesus' broken body. Communion reminds us that we are indeed sacred in the eyes of the Lord.
Does your life line up with your sacredness? What changes do you need to make to move in that direction?

Victory!

Jesus was a casualty of war. It was a spiritual war fought in both the spiritual and physical realm. Jesus was captured. He was tortured. He was executed.

And yet, he was victorious. He triumphed over death.

He defeated the enemy. He is defeating the enemy. He will defeat the enemy. Because of his victory, we too are victorious. Because of his victory, we too will overcome death. Because of his victory, we will dwell with Him in Heaven.

Revelation 21:3-5

3   And I heard a loud voice from the throne saying, "Now the dwelling of God is with men, and he will live with them. They will be his people, and God himself will be with them and be their God.

4   He will wipe every tear from their eyes. There will be no more death or mourning or crying or pain, for the old order of things has passed away."

5   He who was seated on the throne said, "I am making everything new!" Then he said, "Write this down, for these words are trustworthy and true."

The emblems of the Lord's Supper do more than memorialize Jesus' death.

They remind us of Jesus' victory. And thus, they remind us of our destiny.

Sacrifice

I believe that one of the greatest demonstrations of faith seen in the Bible is when Abraham was willing to offer his son as a sacrifice.

Genesis 22:1-2
1   Sometime later God tested Abraham. He said to him, "Abraham!"
"Here I am," he replied.
2   Then God said, "Take your son, your only son, Isaac, whom you love, and go to the region of Moriah. Sacrifice him there as a burnt offering on one of the mountains I will tell you about."

Genesis 22:9-11
9   When they reached the place God had told him about, Abraham built an altar there and arranged the wood on it. He bound his son Isaac and laid him on the altar, on top of the wood.
10   Then he reached out his hand and took the knife to slay his son.
11   But the angel of the LORD called out to him from heaven, "Abraham! Abraham!"
Here I am," he replied.
12   "Do not lay a hand on the boy," he said. "Do not do anything to him. Now I know that you fear God, because you have not withheld from me your son, your only son."

Could you have done that? Would you have been willing to offer your child as a sacrificial offering.
I couldn't. No way.

As a parent, can you imagine the emotions Abraham experienced as he went through this?

And it wasn't a quick thing. Three days' journey out to the point of sacrifice. All the time the thought of losing his beloved son engulfed him.

I believe that this is in the Bible so that we can better understand what God did for us.

John 3:16, "For God so loved the world that he gave his one and only Son, that whoever believes in him shall not perish but have eternal life."

The emblems of the Lord's Supper remind us of the sacrifice your heavenly father has made. They remind us of the emotional turmoil God endured, for three days, when Jesus died for us.

How Many Sins?

How many sins do you suppose you have committed this year?

1 John 1:8, "If we claim to be without sin, we deceive ourselves and the truth is not in us."

If you were able to add them up, what would the total be? Let me give you a few verses to ponder while you do the math:

James 2:9, "But if you show favoritism, you sin and are convicted by the law as lawbreakers."

We tend to think of the big things, but there are also a lot of little things we do that are sinful.

James 4:17, "Therefore, to one who knows the right thing to do, and does not do it, to him it is sin."

Not only are there things we do that we shouldn't do that are sin, but there are things we don't do that we should do that are also sin.

1 John 5:17, "All wrong doing is sin..."

How many sins did you commit this year? (Do you need to borrow a calculator?)
The good news is, regardless of how many sins you have committed, they can all be forgiven.

1 John 1:9, "If we confess our sins, he is faithful and just and will forgive us our sins and purify us from all unrighteousness."

Among other things, the time of communion provides an opportunity to confess our sins to the Lord. After all, that is what His sacrifice is all about.

1 John 4:10, "This is love: not that we loved God, but that he loved us and sent his Son as an atoning sacrifice for our sins."

We are purified of our sins because of the atoning sacrifice of our Lord, Jesus Christ.

Caring for Others

After being arrested, before being crucified, Jesus was beaten, flogged, spat upon, crowned with a crown of thorns, ridiculed, mocked, accused, belittled and then made to carry part of his cross out of the city toward the crucifixion site. Then he was crucified. And yet, even while Jesus was hanging on the cross he was concerned, not about himself, but about his mother.

John 19:25-27

25   Near the cross of Jesus stood his mother, his mother's sister, Mary the wife of Clopas, and Mary Magdalene.
26   When Jesus saw his mother there, and the disciple whom he loved standing nearby, he said to his mother, "Dear woman, here is your son,"
27   and to the disciple, "Here is your mother." From that time on, this disciple took her into his home.

In spite of everything he was going through, Jesus made sure his mother would be cared for after he was gone.

Caring for others. That's the very reason he was on the cross in the first place!

He went to the cross, he died, because he was taking care of us. He was securing for us our salvation.

1 Thessalonians 5:9-10

9   For God did not appoint us to suffer wrath but to receive salvation through our Lord Jesus Christ.
10   He died for us so that, whether we are awake or asleep, we may live together with him.

Even while on the cross Jesus was thinking about his mother. Even while on the cross Jesus was thinking about you and me.

You were, and are, a priority to Jesus. Is He a priority to you?

Big Sin, Little Sin

We've heard that God will punish the wicked. We think of the terrorists and murderers and we think of how evil they are. Compared to them, we're pretty decent folks. We're pretty good.

Let us not deceive ourselves. We are not nearly as bad as they, no comparison, but that doesn't make us good enough.

The fact of the matter is, we've all got our own little sins, and big sins, that God must deal with.

Ecclesiastes 7:20, "There is not a righteous man on earth who does what is right and never sins."

Romans 3:23, "For all have sinned and fall short of the glory of God,"

God is a just God and He will punish all sin. Jesus has already taken your punishment upon Himself. Long before Jesus was crucified, Isaiah prophesied about Jesus' sacrifice:

Isaiah 53:4-6
4   Surely he took up our infirmities and carried our sorrows, yet we considered him stricken by God, smitten by him, and afflicted.
5   But he was pierced for our transgressions, he was crushed for our iniquities; the punishment that brought us peace was upon him, and by his wounds we are healed.
6   We all, like sheep, have gone astray, each of us has turned to his own way; and the LORD has laid on him the iniquity of us all.

God punishes sin. God punishes your sin: big sins and little sins. Jesus took your punishment upon himself. The emblems of the Lord's Supper remind us of the fact that Jesus gave His life for you.

Other books by Don Lawrence

Lessons from Life: 52 Short Devotions
The Book of Revelation: Insights and Interpretations
Murder in a Small Town Church
Shootout at the Soaring Eagle Ranch

Made in the USA
Las Vegas, NV
05 April 2024